MEDIA CONSOLIDATION
AND
NET NEUTRALITY IN THE
U.S.

KARL ROGERS

Media Consolidation and Net Neutrality in the U.S.

In 1919, Theodore Roosevelt warned Americans that international bankers and Rockefeller Standard Oil had taken control over the majority of newspapers and were using this power "to club into submission or drive out of public office officials who refuse to do the bidding of the powerful corrupt cliques which comprise the invisible government." The mayor of New York, John Hylan was quoted in the *New York Times* (March, 26, 1922) as saying that this invisible government was "the real menace to our republic" because "like a giant octopus sprawls its slimy length over city, state, and nation... It seizes in its powerful and long tentacles our executive officers, our legislative bodies, our schools, our courts, our newspapers and everybody created for the public protection." He claimed that "the Rockefeller Standard Oil interest and a small group of private banking houses... practically control both parties, write political platforms, make catspaws of party leaders, use the leading men of private organizations, and resort to every device to place in nomination for high office only such candidates as will be amenable to the dictates of corrupt big business..." Almost a century later, things have not improved. In fact, they have got a lot worse.

Seven corporations now dominate U.S. mass media through media conglomerates. These corporations own all the commercial television networks, all the major Hollywood studios, and most of the cable TV systems and channels. The Federal Communications Commission (FCC) rules on media consolidation allow the same corporation to own both broadcast and print media. This is termed as media-crossover. For example, *News Corporation* is allowed to own Fox News alongside newspapers such as the New York Post and Wall Street Journal, as well as the publisher HarperCollins. Any corporation can buy any form of media, be it satellite TV stations, publishers of school textbooks, radio stations, or Internet websites, as well as sports channels like ESPN. This is termed as media consolidation. These corporations are:

Disney (holdings include: ABC, ESPN, the Disney Channel, Disney XD, A&E and Lifetime, approximately 30 radio stations, music, video game, and book publishing companies, production companies Touchstone, Marvel Entertainment, Lucasfilm, Walt Disney Pictures, Pixar, mobile app developer Disney Mobile, Disney Consumer Products and Interactive Media, and theme parks in several countries. It also has a longstanding partnership with Hearst Corporation, which owns additional TV stations, newspapers, magazines, and stakes in several Disney television ventures);

Time Warner (holdings include CNN, the CW, HBO, Cinemax, Cartoon Network/Adult Swim, HLN, NBA TV, TBS, TNT, truTV, Turner Classic Movies, Warner Bros., Castle Rock, DC Comics, Warner Bros. Interactive Entertainment, New Line Cinema, and Time Magazine);

News Corp (holdings include Fox Broadcasting Company, 20th Century Fox, 21st Century Fox, Fox Searchlight Pictures and Blue Sky Studios, cable networks Fox News Channel, Fox Business Network, Fox Sports 1, Fox Sports 2, Nat Geo Wild, History Channel, FX, FXX, FX Movie Channel, DirecTV, and the regional Fox Sports Networks, and the Dow Jones & Company, Wall Street Journal, New York Post, National Geographic, Barron's, and HarperCollins Publishing);

Viacom (holdings include MTV, Nickelodeon/Nick at Nite, TV Land, VH1, BET, CMT, Comedy Central, Logo TV, Spike, Paramount Pictures, and Paramount Home Entertainment);

CBS (holdings include CBS Television Network, the CW, cable networks CBS Sports Network, Showtime, and Pop, 30 television stations, CBS Radio Inc., which has 130 stations, CBS Television Studios and book publisher Simon & Schuster);

Comcast (through its subsidiary NBC Universal, it owns NBC and Telemundo, Universal Pictures, Illumination Entertainment, Focus Features, DreamWorks Animation, 26 television stations in the United States and cable networks USA Network, Bravo, CNBC, The Weather Channel, MSNBC, Syfy, NBCSN, Golf Channel, Esquire Network, E!, Chiller, Universal HD and the NBC Sports Regional

Networks). Comcast is the largest cable operator and home Internet Service Provider (ISP), and the fourth largest telephone service provider in the United States, providing cable television, broadband Internet, and telephone service to both residential and commercial customers in forty states and the District of Columbia;

Clear Channel Communications is the largest owner of FM and AM radio stations in America, capable of reaching 45 percent of the national audience, as well as owning twelve satellite radio channels, giving it a reach of over 110 million people. These radio stations overwhelmingly promote conservative views and talking points, supporting the GOP in its political campaigns, and criticize the Democratic Party.

The remaining media outlets, such as local newspapers and television stations, are also owned by only a few groups, which are increasingly consolidated into fewer and fewer hands. In May 2017, Sinclair Broadcast Group, based outside Baltimore, announced a $3.9 billion deal to obtain dozens of local television stations by acquiring Tribune Media. This acquisition won approval of the FCC, with only modest concessions, in July and further increases consolidation in the industry. It would offers a greater reach for one of the nation's most conservative media companies.

Sinclair's holdings are vast. It owns or operates more than 170 local television stations and Tribune Media owns 42 television stations in 33 markets, including the nation's top three: New York, Los Angeles and Chicago. With its new holdings, Sinclair would hold stations in seven of the biggest 10 markets. This acquisition would give the company even greater leverage in negotiating deals with the major TV networks whose programming it carries.

Seemingly independent commercial online media ventures, such as the movie and TV video streaming website Hulu, are jointly owned by News Corp, the Walt Disney Company, and Comcast. Netflix is a competitor to Hulu. It is not beyond the realm of imagination that Comcast could charge Netflix higher fees to use the Internet or even slow or block its transmissions, in order to give Hulu an advantage. Actually, Brian Stelter of *The New York Times*, Marguerite Reardon of *CNET News*, and Seth Weintraub have reported that Comcast has already done exactly that.[1] We can imagine that these stories would not have been published if Comcast owned *The New York Times*, *CNET*, and *CNN*. This is why media consolidation, especially involving mergers between telecom giants and media conglomerates, should be of public concern.

As of February 2017, AT&T and Time Warner are in talks to merge into one super-conglomerate creating the largest telecommunications, mass media, and entertainment corporation in the United States. The deal is said to be "imminent" after the FCC declined to review it.

Why is this a problem? Media consolidation has resulted in fewer and fewer people owning mass media. As a result, mass media represent a narrower range of interests, with ultimately the bottom-line of profit being the dominant interest.[2] The marketplace of ideas has become a marketplace, full stop. Sound bites and punditry have become the norm—as news is interwoven with entertainment, propaganda, and advertising—as ad revenues take precedence over the public interest. Ratings dominate. Both free speech and investigative journalism have suffered as a result, as well as local news coverage, transparency of government, and public debate during elections. In the political sphere, perception is power. This gives media conglomerates power over politicians. The owners of media corporations have become the "gatekeepers" for the nomination and election of candidates to the extent that they decide who or what is covered, and they raise the cost of media access for candidates when running for election to public office. Political parties have to raise a lot of money to run a corporate media based political campaign—for advertising, interviews, favorable editorials and punditry—and they raise this money from corporations and other big business interests. The party faithful from both the Republican and Democratic parties and the electorate in general only gets to choose between corporate-vetted candidates who, regardless of what positions they take on abortion, marriage, religion, or guns, are pro-corporate candidates, funded by PACs and Super PACs.

The Center for Responsive Politics reported that business interests contributed over $1.23 billion in the 2000 elections, and $1.03 billion in the 2002 mid-term elections.[3] The candidate who

4

raised the most money won 94% of all elections. Business accounts for 73.3% of all campaign spending. In contrast, organized labor unions only account for 7%. The total campaign spending on the 2004 and 2008 elections were 4.1 and 5.2 billion dollars, respectively. The spending on the 2012 and 2016 U.S. elections topped 6 billion dollars each.

Media consolidation should also be of public concern also when a non-media parent corporation can effectively use its media holdings to suppress any news or criticism to protect its own public image. For example, the *New York Times* (Jan, 21, 1983) reported that in the early 1980s General Electric used its media holdings to cover up that it had polluted the Hudson River.[4] It is also of public concern when a non-media parent corporation can use its media holdings to support a candidate for public office and attack his or her opponents if that candidate agrees to do its lobbyists' bidding.[5] Lobbyists use millions of dollars of their clients' money to buy access to congresspersons. Politicians are funded by corporations to attend "fact finding" weekends or conferences. These kinds of activities do not have to be reported in accordance with the 1995 Lobbying Disclosure Act. Lobbyists also remind politicians that they have to worry about re-election; corporate money is required, given the increased costs of running for public office. And there is always the promise of opportunities in the future, after retiring from public office. Former CEOs and corporate lawyers are appointed to head the very same federal agencies involved in regulating their former business, or even sit on the Supreme Court. This forms something of a revolving door of conflicts of interest, which has rolled back environmental and consumer protections, privatized schools and prisons, increased corporate spending on campaigns for state judicial elections of judges and attorneys general, struck down state and citywide labor protection laws, and abused eminent domain to force citizens to sell their private property to corporate developers.[6] Lobbyists also work ceaselessly to influence federal regulatory agencies like the FCC and Federal Election Commission (FEC) to interpret and apply legislation in a way that benefits their corporate clients. Sometimes lobbyists are able to persuade regulatory agencies to postpone the application and enforcement of legislation or regulations. The pressures on the FCC and FEC are enormous. Even when hard-fought citizens' campaigns for public protections and oversight have been won, laws are often subverted, diluted, stalled, or simply not enforced. Legislators and high-ranking officials have been known to sit on committees regulating their own business interests and many have financial ties to the businesses lobbying them.[7]

In the days after the September 2001 terrorist attacks, Sinclair instructed the news and sports anchors (and even weather forecasters!) to read editorial messages explicitly conveying full support for the Bush administration's fight against terrorism, despite objections raised by editors and staffers. In early 2004, Sinclair sent a reporting crew to Iraq, including its chief editorialist whose conservative commentaries are carried on dozens of Sinclair stations, in search of "overlooked" stories with a more positive spin in favor of the war. Sinclair declined to broadcast a special from Nightline on its seven ABC stations, because it ascribed anti-war motivations to anchor Ted Koppel's plan to read the names of all U.S. service members who had been killed in Iraq. Later that year, former Sinclair Washington bureau chief Jon Leiberman openly opposed plans to air an hour-long program in the height of election season attacking Democratic nominee John Kerry for his service record in Vietnam and his anti-war stances afterward. Leiberman told David Folkenflik (NPR) in an interview that he had voted for George W. Bush in 2000 but under Sinclair his show had become "biased political propaganda, with clear intentions to sway this election." The company fired Leiberman the day after his interview, saying he was a disgruntled employee.

In 2012, the company paid for robo-calls taped by one of Sinclair's Baltimore anchors to be placed to households around Maryland with questions loaded against the positions of then Democratic Gov. Martin O'Malley. In 2016, Sinclair directed stations to carry certain "must-run" stories that reflected poorly on Democratic nominee Hillary Clinton. Stories on Republican nominee Donald Trump were largely sympathetic or neutral, according to the newspaper. In December, Politico reported that Jared Kushner had boasted to business executives that the Trump campaign had struck a deal giving access to Sinclair in exchange for more favorable coverage, a claim the chain denied. However, in 2017, Sinclair signed former Trump campaign aide Boris Epshteyn as its chief political analyst. To lead its Sunday public affairs show, Sinclair hired former CBS correspondent Sharyl Atkisson, an investigative reporter whose scrutiny of the Obama administration won her the admiration of many conservatives. Sinclair has announced a possible conversion of Tribune's WGN America as a conservative news and opinion channel.

Corporations also hire the services of public relations firms, opinion pollsters, trade associations, think tanks, policy centers, and campaigners to bombard politicians with pro-corporate propaganda, while threatening capital flight or withdrawing support for any politician or candidate who does not play ball. The Internet is awash with "think tanks" and "policy centers" offering biased and selective research and polls. Lobbyists and media pundits can pick the research findings that give them the conclusions they want. Many of these "think tanks" and "policy centers" have been purposely built to give credibility and the illusion of corroboration to the desired conclusions. These "research findings" and "poll results" make their way into seemingly independent media sources—that are also owned by the same corporations that fund the "think tanks" and "policy centers." Donation filtering services on the Internet allow sources of funding to be concealed, also allowing corporations to fund "independent film-makers" to produce documentaries that just-so-happen to defend the industry and discredit its critics. Propaganda and counter-propaganda take the place of informed debate and open-minded inquiry.

Hired "experts" often dominate public hearings and media, using manufactured facts or statistics provided by manufactured sources, or using marginal findings in attempts to discredit areas of massive scientific consensus. These marginal findings are given disproportionate levels of coverage in corporate owned newspapers, radio, and television, alongside reiteration and supporting commentary in apparently independent Internet sources, such as blogs, online journals, documentaries, social media networks, which have been constructed for the sole purpose of providing this level of social reinforcement and publicity. Meanwhile, TV and radio pundits reinforce the message and discredit its critics. Actual scientific research is ignored or given scant coverage, and when the "marginal findings" have either been discredited by scientists or shown to be manufactured propaganda, this information is suppressed and ignored. Lies, distortions, and distractions dominate the airwaves and print, alongside the power to prevent the public from learning the facts or truth about anything that it is in the interest of the owners of media to cover-up.

No better example of this can be found in the seemingly tireless attempts by Fox News to construct "scientific controversy" in the case of global warming caused by industrial pollution, which seems to extend to their concern about any area of regulatory oversight that might have an impact on profits and shareholder dividends. While there may be some Fox News viewers who are sufficiently ill-informed to believe that Fox News really is "fair and balanced," others are aware that Fox News reporting is biased. All news reporting is biased. Yet there is a distinction to be made between bias, in the sense of reflecting a point of view, and deliberately misleading a target audience.[8] This is further compounded by the fact that corporate media no longer investigates or even checks the statements of fact. Any statement is admissible if it corroborates the message of the day. Pundits just run with whatever narrative suits their paymasters' agenda—perhaps later reversing, changing, or simply dropping it, as and when needed. Repeatedly, without evidence, scientists will be described as conspirators working for World Government or perpetrating a global hoax. Every time a guest mentions "global warming," the host immediately repeats the phrase "scientific controversy" and talks over the guest—while leaving their narrowcasted audience to continue in a state of denial and ignorance about climate change. When scientists come to the "wrong" conclusion that acts against corporate interests, media criticism of that conclusion quickly follows, using little more than innuendo and slander to discredit scientists. On the other hand, if an isolated and uncorroborated scientific paper just so happens to agree with the message of the day, it is flaunted as definitive proof for all time. Hearings or proposed laws in Congress are usually reported, if at all, only when it is far too late for the public to have any influence on the legislature—unless that legislation is to provide any kind of environmental protection or regulation, in which case it is attacked and vilified as "a Big Government takeover" that "will cost jobs" whatever the proposed protection might be.

8

This does not necessarily require any massive conspiracy. Once we recognize that corporations are only driven by the imperative to lower costs and maximize profits, we have to accept that media corporations have to appease their sponsors and owners rather than serve the public need for information. Media outlets provide "off-the-rack" sound-bites and talking-points, according to the needs of their sponsors and owners. Access to media becomes increasing expensive. When an oligopoly dominates the market, only the interests of media owners and investors are represented; competition, innovation, and the public interest suffer as a result. Increased prices and poorer levels of customer service soon follow, as the share price becomes the bottom line in an international investors' market, along with less media diversity, the loss of the freedom of the press, greater corporate influence over government, further deregulation and consolidation, and a poorly informed or increasingly misinformed public. Pundits on corporate media channels can say whatever they please in the run up to elections, and any corporation or organization can buy ad time to run whatever campaign ads or infomercials that they please, and apparently independent exposés of candidates can receive disproportionate coverage and airtime, alongside supporting and reinforcing chatter on the Internet. Attack ads, petitions, and protests against a candidate or proposition can be run by any group set up by a corporation, presenting itself as a concerned citizens group, a think tank, an institution, or an association. Mass media campaigns make or break a candidate, especially given that for most people the only things they know about their representative or senator is what they have seen about him or her on TV, heard on radio, or read in newspapers. Media corporations have a troubling level of influence over political campaigns, given that they have the power to silence a candidate, to select what to cover and when to cover it, or to editorialize for or against candidates, and this is even more troubling when they blatantly lie to an increasingly narrowcasted audience. Given that corporations spend billions of dollars on campaigning and lobbying, why is it surprising that corporations have come to dominate politics at every level? It would be surprising if they didn't.

If the task of media is to act as a watchdog on governmental policies and the activities of the wealthy and powerful—as a watchdog on corruption and power—then the mainstream media have failed. However, as a megaphone for the rich and powerful—a multimedia propaganda machine—then corporate media is very successful indeed. The basic problem is straightforward. As long as politicians need huge sums of money to get elected and re-elected, they will inevitably pander to whoever foots the bill, and while media corporations can be owned by parent corporations, they will inevitably serve their parent corporation's interests. The political problem facing America is one of a struggle for political accountability—how to make the so-called representatives of the people accountable to the people, rather than to powerful corporations and the economic elite. This is a struggle over sovereignty versus ownership. Who governs America? Control over mass media is central to this struggle and its outcome will define the future of America.

Citizens' campaigns for changes in laws and regulations are often frustrated by the fact that all three branches of government and the mainstream media are already dominated by corporations and corporate interests. With increased media consolidation, a great deal of local, state, and federal governmental processes, such as the work of regulatory agencies and legislatures, are simply ignored— unless they corroborate the message or talking points of the day. This leaves crucial operations of government uncovered by media and erodes the possibility of public oversight and political accountability. Through the use of PACs, corporations are increasingly dominating the funding of the campaigns to elect judges (38 states have judicial elections) and influence the nomination and appointment of federal judges. Organizations like the US Chamber of Commerce, the National Chamber Litigation Center, the Washington Legal Foundation, and the Federalist Society have actively funded, promoted, and advanced a pro-corporate agenda within the courts and legal system. This not only involves advocating or opposing new regulations and legislation, but also rolling back long-established laws and regulations for which there is widespread consensus, such as health-and-safety-at-work laws, or anti-discrimination laws. Of course, this state of affairs benefits the corporations who have hijacked the political process in order to gain a favorable regulatory environment, tax breaks, government contracts, and friends in high places.

10

It is for this reason that the citizens' campaigns cannot rely on Congress to pass comprehensive campaign finance reform that can remove corruption from politics and the Supreme Court to uphold it. The 1972 Federal Election Campaign Act (which compelled disclosures of campaign contributions) and the forming of the FEC to enforce it was effectively subverted in 1975 when the FEC ruled that corporations were allowed to organize PACs to collect and bundle shareholder and employee campaign contributions, as well as also use corporate funds for campaign advertising in favor of a particular candidate or against their opposition *without requiring shareholder approval.* Spending other people's money was equated with free speech. The door was opened to corporations to dominate elections. This was bolstered by Buckley v Valeo, the 1976 Supreme Court ruling that any imposed limits on campaign expenditures was unconstitutional.[9] The door was wedged open. And in 2010, in the landmark case Citizens United v FEC, the Supreme Court ruled that unlimited campaign expenditure should be allowed on the grounds of the First Amendment, and that the prohibition on corporate- and union- funded political broadcasts within 60 days of a federal election or 30 days of a primary election was unconstitutional.[10] The door had come off its hinges. Not only did this weaken the 2002 Bipartisan Campaign Reform Act, which banned "soft money" donations for "party building" as well as imposed restrictions on election broadcast ads on the run up to elections and primaries. It also announced that the Supreme Court was deaf to concerns about political corruption and charges of judicial activism, and it also announced that precedent was not considered binding. The corporations won their day in court.

Is propaganda free speech? Most of us know that mass media propaganda works—especially in the run-up to elections (otherwise what would be the point of spending millions of dollars on it?) A free press cannot exist when it is controlled by only a few people with shared commercial interests at stake to whom politicians owe their election and re-election. Propaganda works and money corrupts politics. No amount of campaign reform will make any significant progress towards free and fair elections without a free press. The corporate domination of mass media and influence over elections—by equating money and speech—has stifled the freedom of speech of the many millions of Americans who have concerns and problems other than maximizing profits and increasing shareholder dividends. When Congressmen have become deaf to the concerns of their constituents, they no longer represent them. They represent those who pay for their election and re-election, and those who offer them lucrative employment and positions on boards of directors after they have left public office. For as long as they need to be elected and re-elected, while continuing to ignore their constituents, self-serving politicians will use the propaganda machine to defame or silence their opponents or, if need be, scare the hell out of their constituents.

Nevertheless, according to the Supreme Court, there is no way to distinguish PR firms on Madison Avenue and multibillion dollar media conglomerates from the free press of eighteenth century Massachusetts or Pennsylvania. SCOTUS ignored the fact that all this money flooding into elections has raised the cost of political campaigning; putting it further out of most citizens' reach and therefore Congress has a compelling interest (supported by Article I, section 5 of the Constitution) in placing limits on election expenditure. Whether government can place limits on propaganda outlets like Citizens United was considered by SCOTUS to be only a freedom of speech issue. Not only was there apparently no way to distinguish propaganda from free speech in the mind of the Supreme Court, but there was even a refusal to consider the question of whether any distinction was possible. Money is speech. Corporations enjoy the First Amendment right to free speech—the right to spend money disseminating propaganda—regardless of the identity of the speaker. In the world of corporate media, advertising, political candidates, news, and media punditry are products, same as soup or hats, yet they somehow maintain their special position as "the free press" of the First Amendment. Yet the most pernicious implication of SCOTUS's ruling is that bribery and corruption are now protected by law, while political speech, advertising, and propaganda are blended together and transmitted through TV and radio into millions of homes and workplaces.

It is obviously absurd to treat multinational corporate media conglomerates as if they are the same as the free press of the eighteenth century to which the First Amendment refers. With increased economic leverage comes increased political importance and influence—and with share ownership and limited liability, mass media can hardly be considered to be "free" when it can be owned and the bottom-line is increased share value. Add increased audience reach and a century of public relations into the admixture of money and politics and we have a very different state of affairs than those days of printing press, paper, and ink, limited in circulation to those who could read. When the First Amendment was written in 1789, anyone with a printing press, ink, and paper could become part of "the press" to which the amendment refers. Today, billionaires own all the newspapers and presses, along with corporate TV, radio, and movie studios. This kind of media conglomerate is not "the free press." It is a money-making enterprise run for profit and power, with shares floated on international stock markets. Out of cut-throat necessity, the competitive world of international investors' markets, wherein investors demand the highest return on their investment or they will invest their money elsewhere, places the interests of the shareholders and next quarterly profit report at a much higher priority in the minds of CEOs and Boards of Directors than respecting the conditions for a free press, the public good, and the best interests of the citizenry in general. News and editorials need to be as mainstream and uncontroversial as possible to avoid offending sponsors and advertisers, and losing revenue leads to lower share value. Investigative journalism is expensive, risks lawsuits and the disfavor of corrupt politicians, and reduces profits. Local news is expensive and has a lower market share of audience and sponsors. By blurring the line between news and entertainment, ratings go up. Gossip, sleaze, celebrities, and sensationalism sell. Sex and violence sell. Quick sound bites and slogans trump journalism and in-depth reporting. Media corporations are reactionary. In a real sense, they do give the public what they want—as well as make sure that people have very few alternatives.

Is there anything we can do about it? We can turn it off. We can also recall that the public owns the airwaves. The 1927 Radio Act nationalized the airwaves and formed the Federal Radio Commission (FRC) to oversee the licensing of radio stations. The FRC was charged with protecting the public interest and "the emphasis must be first and foremost on the interest, the convenience, and the necessity of the listening public, and not on the interest, convenience, or necessity of the individual broadcaster or the advertiser." The FRC was replaced by the FCC when the 1934 Communications Act was passed to regulate the telephone companies and the FCC was charged with preserving "the public interest, convenience, and necessity" when handing out licenses for radio stations. The FCC policy was that it would not be in the public's interest for a single entity to hold more than one broadcast license in the same community. The public would benefit from a diverse array of owners because it would lead to a diverse array of programs and viewpoints. The Communications Act empowered the FCC to impose penalties and regulate standards and equipment used on the airwaves, as well as award licenses. The largest radio operators at that time, ABC and NBC, lobbied for high license fees to cut down on competition, but the FCC ruled that this would hinder free speech, so it gave out licenses free of charge, providing the licensee agreed to protect "the public interest, convenience, and necessity" and provide news programs.

In 1975, the FCC banned cross-ownership of full-power TV, radio stations, and newspapers in order to maintain media diversity and in recognition of the value and scarcity of the public airwaves. This state of affairs continued until the 1996 Telecommunications Act allowed media mergers and consolidation, and instructed the FCC to review its rules accordingly. In June 2003, the FCC repealed the 1975 ban on cross-ownership, without allotting the required period of time for public comments and, in 2007, the FCC agreed to consider relaxing its rules on media ownership even further "on a case by case basis."[11] While Congress is culpable for putting the interests of corporations over the wider public interest, clearly the FCC is no longer in the business of "protecting the public interest, convenience, and necessity." So, who will protect the public interest?

We need to look in the mirror. We watch TV, listen to radio, and read newspapers. We are the reason companies advertise on TV, radio, and in newspapers. The public still owns the airwaves (which are leased to corporations) and politicians have a duty to remind licensees that they have a legal obligation to serve "the public interest, convenience, and necessity." Who is going to compel politicians to perform their duty? People need to demand that Congress and the FCC makes sure that the publicly owned airwaves are used in the public interest, whatever the public deem that to be, and review licenses for public interest considerations. What can we do? Pressure Congress to compel the FCC to reverse its course of deregulation, tighten and enforce the rules on media ownership, increase media diversity, and review licenses for the public interest.

Free Press, a public advocacy group launched in 2002, has called on Congress and the FCC to protect the public interest. This group advocates democratic media reform and for the press to act as a watchdog on the government, corporate media conglomerates, and big moneyed interests.[12] Co-founder Robert McChesney remarked:

"[I]n the next five to 10 years, if not less, fundamental communication policy decisions likely will be made that will shape our nation for decades, maybe generations. Whether we will even have something remotely close to a credible journalism is very much up for grabs, along with much else. These decisions will be made whether we like it or not, under terms over which we have only a little control. If we elect to sit this one out because we are unable to get the ideal results in the short-term, or because this movement does not score high enough on our checklist of core issues, we "ain't going to make it with anyone anyhow." We will simply be fools."[13]

In 2003, a public advocacy group called *the Prometheus Radio Project* took the FCC to the Third Circuit Court of Appeals, which ruled 2-1 that the FCC needed to re-evaluate its new rules for weakening the restrictions on ownership and remove the "irrational assumptions and inconsistencies" in its determination of the level of media diversity.[14] FCC Commissioner Michael Copps opposed the FCC ruling (June, 2, 2003) and stated that these new rules had undermined the whole democratic process and the free press in America. After that ruling, he argued that only a few corporations would be the gatekeepers of all civil dialogue in America, and that these corporations would have "veto power" over what Americans watch, listen to, or read. *Even the US Senate* took the FCC to task over this ruling as clearly against the public best interest and in favor of corporate interests. SCOTUS refused to hear the FCC's appeal. As a result, the FCC redrew its rules and promised to wait for the public submission of comments, ten commissioned reports, and six public hearings in order to demonstrate that it had figured in the public interest and concerns before making any rule changes. After reviewing the case in 2010, the court lifted its stay on the FCC rules. The FCC has since ignored its own redrawn rules and continued on a path of deregulation, permitting further media consolidation.

Michael Powell, Chairman of the FCC (2001-2005), is on the record as having said that he had "no idea what the public interest is" and that "the oppressor here is regulation."[15] Powell is a longtime member of the Republican Party and lobbyist for telecommunication industry deregulation. He resigned as Chairman of the FCC in 2005. Since April, 25, 2011, he has become the president of the National Cable & Telecommunications Association. Here we see how the revolving door of politics works. The myth of deregulation is that deregulation results in fewer rules. This is not the case. What "deregulation" really means is that the old rules are replaced with a new set of rules that better serve the interests of the industries or businesses that have lobbied for these new rules. What many Americans do not realize is that rulings such as the FCC ruling on June, 2, 2003 and the SCOTUS ruling on Citizens United are not independent. They are the consequences of corporate dominance over all three branches of government and the press. The links between corporate media, telecommunications giants, the FCC, Congress, the Administration, and SCOTUS have been carefully wrought through the revolving door of appointments and lobbying. Corporations can conceal their donations and lobbying activities through organizations such as the Heritage Foundation, the Cato Institute, the American Enterprise Institute, the US Chamber of Commerce, and the Federalist Society to influence nominations and appointments. These organizations have worked together to have pro-corporate judges nominated and appointed to SCOTUS, as well as in state and district courts, and have helped pro-corporate politicians be elected to Congress and as President, and also had advocates of "deregulation" appointed to key positions in the Administration (such as the FCC and FEC). They also run their own propaganda campaigns to disguise the corporate takeover of America as "deregulation," "globalization," and "the free market."

Clearly the American people need to take this issue seriously and petition their representatives and senators to force the FCC to protect the public interest. Congress needs to force the FCC to do its job. What is also needed is for Congress to enact antitrust legislation to break up media conglomerates, reintroduce media competition and diversity, and prevent non-media corporations from owning media. This would widen the ownership of media and avoid conflicts between commercial interests and the public interest. This is not the same as government control over media. It is a matter of wider private ownership of media sources by increasing market competition and a wider diversity of points of view, giving more people an opportunity own media and to shape the political process. It would allow more dissenting voices to be heard by anyone who wants to listen to them; to present alternatives, to bring different things to the public attention and to inform people more thoroughly about the activities of the government and big moneyed interests. This is essential for free speech and a free press. Without a free press, how can the public be politically informed, critical, and democratic?

The existence of an informed public is essential for political accountability, transparency, and equality of all under the law. These are the pillars of a republic, as well as necessary for democracy and good government, and the reason why the press is included in the First Amendment and considered as the fourth branch of government, or "the Fourth Estate." When informed by a free press, the people can act as a check and balance to government and corporate power.

However, broadening the range of private media ownership is not enough. Alongside greater diversity in privately owned media, there needs to be better-funded public media—such as PBS and NPR—to provide low-cost or free public media coverage of the political process, from local school board elections to presidential elections, and every committee and commission in between, with channels providing local, state, and national 24-hour coverage on TV, radio, the Internet, and emergency channels. Greater funding for public access media is also needed, which gives ordinary people the opportunity to produce and control the content of their own television and radio shows. PBS and NPR should also have a highly developed Internet presence accessible through both home and wireless connections. PBS and NPR should provide 24-hour multi-channel, multimedia coverage of campaigns during the run-up to primaries and elections. PBS and NPR should be required to also give equal airtime to all the political candidates in debates and interviews in the run-up to an election, which would give better opportunities for third party and independent candidates to be heard and seen by the electorate, opening up the possibility of multiparty elections and grassroots challenges to incumbents. Free airtime for candidates, strictly enforced spending limits, and public funding for election campaigns would reduce candidates' need for corporate donations, allowing a wider range of interests and concerns to be represented during elections. PBS and NPR should act as a counterbalance to corporate influence on campaign spending that occurs in for-profit corporate media.

By an act of Congress, PBS and NPR could also be first to present the official results and private news channels should be prohibited by law from "calling the results"—effectively putting an end to the dubious corporate media practice of "calling" elections based on exit poll data—although the First Amendment right to free speech should be unrestrained once the official results have been called.

Funding for PBS and NPR could be raised by actually charging corporations licensing fees to use the public airwaves and enforce the "must carry" obligations of TV and radio companies to provide for the public interest by carrying PBS and NPR programs. Both PBS and NPR should also run their own stations and when doing so should be given the option to carry commercial (non-political) advertising to make them self-funded and non-profit, spending revenues on improving and maintaining equipment, and providing a free media service across America. In this way, every American could follow closely the political and electoral process, as it happens at every level and branch of government, at local and national levels, without costing the taxpayers a dime. The American public would be better placed to understand the political process and, as a constituent or member of an organization, to petition government.

However, can we really expect Congress to do these things? After all, aren't they just as much in the pockets of corporations as the FCC and SCOTUS? In 2017, the new administration announced it plans to slash funding for NPR and PBS. In the absence of better-funded public media, the Internet remains the last bastion of the free press. We need to create better media for ourselves using the

Internet to educate ourselves, share experiences and ideas, inform and communicate with each other, and organize ourselves to be better placed to participate in the political process. The growing shift towards Internet-based media, alongside increasing public awareness that corporate media disseminates propaganda and misinformation, provides the impetus for the democratic reform of media. People are turning off corporate television and talk radio, and logging on to social media and video sharing networks, sharing alternative media sources providing online news, making documentaries, joining political campaigns, organizing petitions, protests, boycotts, and strikes, and funding grassroots campaigns for election to public office and voter initiatives. The virtue of the Internet is that it is participatory to the extent that anyone with a computer, modem, and an ISP can join in and connect with other people and groups. Through the Internet, people can organize grassroots political campaigns to pressure politicians to call for or oppose new legislation and, in some states, people can organize referenda or recalls of elected politicians.

The Internet also provides the means for grassroots political campaigning for anyone to run for public office and communicate with voters. Due to the low cost of using the Internet, grassroots campaigns can effectively counter corporate media propaganda by providing people with information and the opportunity to educate themselves on candidates and the issues that matter to them. Through Internet-based grassroots campaigns and democratic participation, third parties and independent candidates can effectively run against corporate-backed Republican or Democrat incumbents. The democratization of the Internet, as the technology by which this new free press can operate as a watchdog on the political process, offers people the potential for the democratization of the political process and representative government. Coming together, building and maintaining a participatory, democratic, and open Internet is the next frontier in the struggle between democratic and corporate America.

Can Internet-based media really pressure politicians? The massive grassroots Internet-based media backlash against SOPA and PIPA in early 2012 showed that it can.[16] As a result of Internet-based campaigns, petitions, blackouts, and the threat of boycotts and protests, Congress stalled the vote on these bills. Corporate media had been conspicuously silent about these proposed laws, yet people were able to use the Internet to bring SOPA and PIPA to public attention. This shows the power of the Internet to act as a medium for the people to act as a free press, learn what is going on in the world, share information and experiences, and participate in the political process through organizations and campaigns. This is how democracy works. However, governmental and corporate struggles for control over the Internet continued. Instead, the Senate pushed ahead with the greatly weakened and amended Cybersecurity Act, which granted both telecommunications corporations and the government the authority to deny access to the Internet on the grounds of "national security" and also to impose conditions and compliance costs, such as running approved "security" software and equipment. In 2015 the Cybersecurity Act was amended to allow interagency sharing of information regarding security threats to infrastructure and control systems, and in 2017 amendments to the Cybersecurity Act are in congressional committee to implement measures to protect public traded companies, providing that First Amendment rights are not violated.

However, although already signed by the United States, along with 30 countries worldwide, in 2012 the Anti-Counterfeiting Trade Agreement (ACTA) was ratified by governments of the European Union, despite massive protests and public opposition.[17] This treaty effectively hands over the right of access to the Internet to collaborations between telecommunications and media corporations, with little in the way of government oversight and no clear mechanism of appeal by users who are denied Internet access on the grounds of "copyright infringement." Not content with ACTA, the Motion Pictures Association of America, the Recording Industry Association of America, and Internet Service Providers have come to "a voluntary agreement" to establish a "graduated response" to punish users for "copyright infringement," which would include sharing any files or parts of files for which copyright is asserted by members of the MPAA and RIAA, without any mechanism for appeal. Does this constitute a reasonable protection of copyright, or is it just another attempt to use "copyright protection" as a way to seize control over the Internet?

20

It is for this reason that net neutrality must be defended against relentless assaults from corporate lobbyists and lawyers. And it is for this same reason that net neutrality will face relentless assaults from corporate lobbyists, the courts, and the corporate propaganda machine. Media pundits and propagandists claim that net neutrality is code for government control over the Internet, but it must be emphasized from the outset that this is one of the many lies about net neutrality that corporate media propagandists have been spreading.[18] What does net neutrality mean?

"...messages received from any individual, company, or corporation, or from any telegraph lines connecting with this line at either of its termini, shall be impartially transmitted in the order of their reception, excepting that the dispatches of the government shall have priority." —Pacific Telegraph Act, 1860

Co-inventor of the Internet, Bob Kahn has expressed concerns about the Internet becoming fragmented or damaged due to government regulation, but he has also warned us against using the term "net neutrality" as merely a slogan.[19] So, let's not do that. What is net neutrality? Put simply, net neutrality is the principle that no restrictions on data transmission speed and content are imposed on the Internet by anyone, neither governments nor corporations, and all legal data must be treated equally by ISPs. Net neutrality guarantees that ISPs are not allowed to discriminate between types or sources of data. All sources of Internet data traffic should be treated equally. Content is decided by the users of the Internet, not by telecommunications corporations acting as gatekeepers or owners. It is quite simply "a first come, first served" process of dealing with transmitted data. More specifically, net neutrality means that ISPs cannot slow down the rate of data transmission or block sources to create a tiered Internet that would allow them to charge higher fees to use the faster rate of transmission or block competitors. Regulation based on the principle of net neutrality would not be the imposition of government control or "the Fairness Doctrine," as some corporate media pundits have suggested,[20] but would prevent telecommunication corporations from restricting people's access to the Internet, blocking competitors, or limiting the types of platform, coding, or equipment used. Since its invention, the Internet has been based on a principle of net neutrality and what critics of net neutrality want is the opportunity for telecom and media corporations to make more money by controlling people's access to the Internet. As Tim Wu put it,

"Network neutrality is best defined as a network design principle. The idea is that a maximally useful public information network aspires to treat all content, sites, and platforms equally."[21]

It is as simple as that.

Net neutrality requires that Internet users can equally share, upload and download content and use the Internet without ISP prejudice. It requires that people can freely explore the Internet—an extension of the freedom of association, as well as freedom of speech. People need to have equal and affordable access to the Internet. Just as telephone companies are not permitted to tell callers who they can call or what they can say, broadband carriers should not be allowed to use their market power to control who Internet users contact and what they share. ISPs should not be able to screen, filter, or block data. When critics of net neutrality—such as the Cato Institute and the Ayn Rand Institute—argue that free market competition and quality of service would discourage telecommunications corporations from data discrimination, and, therefore, the industry can be trusted to self-regulate, they seem to require that we suspend all disbelief and just have faith. This faith denies the facts of the record of these corporations and also how corporate mergers have placed a great deal of power over the Internet in the hands of fewer and fewer people. It also denies the fact that corporations can come to "voluntary agreements" and establish a monopolistic control over Internet traffic—while Congress and the FCC fail to enforce anti-trust legislation. It is simply naïve or dishonest to claim that these corporations can be trusted not to put their own short-term interests first and foremost.

What net neutrality requires is that the Internet remains decentralized and uncontrolled, thereby making it impossible for anyone to take over or shut down the Internet. In a democracy, media competition and diversity are essential to provide the level of pluralism and free speech needed to counter the propaganda machine. Media conglomerates oppose the freedom of the press and diverse public debate when either threatens corporate profits. Net neutrality advocates claim that government should play only a regulatory role, by enforcing antitrust legislation to prevent a few conglomerates from owning the Internet and controlling both its rate of data transmission and content. If a conglomerate controls both the pipeline and the data that passes through it, then a loss in market competition and abuses of power will inevitably result. The market of ideas and public debate depend on media diversity, competition, and freedom. In many respects, America has turned full circle back to the early twentieth century progressive call for trust busting! It is for this reason that the FCC approval of Comcast and General Electric owning NBC (including MSNBC, Universal, and Telemundo) does not bode well for the future of net neutrality. This ruling by the FCC is yet another example of how the government serves corporate interests, rather than those of the people. It turns the Internet over to predatory capitalism and corporate consolidation.

Still, we still need to answer one important question. What of the protection of copyright? This question is at the heart of proposed laws such as PIPA and SOPA, and treaties such as ACTA. My own answer is that the entertainment industry needs to change their business model in order to incorporate that copyright infringement and the uncontrollable sharing of music and film via the Internet are now facts of life. They need to adapt to the Internet, rather than impose the right to decide who can access and use it. Enforcement methods will inevitably stifle freedom of speech, the freedom of the press, and technological innovation, without stopping piracy, and unfairly penalize Internet users and companies on an ad hoc and ineffectual basis. Just as international regional codes for DVDs did not stop piracy, neither will partitioning the Internet into regional zones under the control of different governments and cartels of corporations. Copyright enforcement should be strictly limited to the sale of copyrighted material, and conducted according to the laws and international treaties regarding commercial transactions. It should not penalize users for freely sharing data, nor the websites that facilitate these exchanges, but focus its attention on websites and businesses that are illegally selling copyrighted material, and fair use for intellectual, journalistic, and scientific use should be strictly protected, along with the freedom of speech and expression. It seems to me that the entertainment industry should change its business model to offer high quality and secure online downloads of music and film to subscribers, receiving a fee from subscribers to access their sites, and accept that copying and sharing will occur. To partition the Internet to prevent file sharing is simply using a hammer to crack a nut and governments should not allow a powerful lobby like the entertainment industry to threaten to serious disrupt the flow of data, just simply to preserve its old business model and profits.

After Powell left in 2005, the FCC adopted a policy statement[22] stating

"As Congress has noted, '[t]he rapidly developing array of Internet . . . services available to individual Americans represent an extraordinary advance in the availability of educational and informational resources to our citizens.'"

And

"The Internet also represents a forum for a true diversity of political discourse, unique opportunities for cultural development, and myriad avenues for intellectual activity."

And

"In addition, the Internet plays an important role in the economy, as an engine for productivity growth and cost savings."

And

"In section 230(b) of the Communications Act of 1934, as amended (Communications Act or Act), Congress describes its national Internet policy. Specifically, Congress states that it is the policy of the United States to preserve the vibrant and competitive free market that presently exists for the Internet and to promote the continued development of the Internet."

And

"In section 706(a) of the Act, Congress charges the Commission with "encourag[ing] the deployment on a reasonable and timely basis of advanced telecommunications capability" – broadband – "to all Americans."

24

The FCC also stated that it adhered to four principles of network neutrality to "encourage broadband deployment and preserve and promote the open and interconnected nature of the public Internet". These four principles were as follows:

1. Consumers are entitled to access the lawful Internet content of their choice.
2. Consumers are entitled to run applications and use services of their choice, subject to the needs of law enforcement.
3. Consumers are entitled to connect their choice of legal devices that do not harm the network.
4. Consumers are entitled to competition among network providers, application and service providers, and content providers.

In 2008, Kevin Martin, as the Chairman of the FCC, announced that he was "ready, willing and able to prevent broadband ISPs from irrationally interfering with their subscribers' Internet access."[23] This came four months after Comcast was found to have been blocking or delaying BiTorrent data; Comcast, without admitting any wrongdoing, agreed to be neutral regarding protocol and data management. Even though FCC policy statements are not legally binding and this was the first time the FCC had ruled in an ISP management decision, in August 2008, the FCC ruled that Comcast had interfered with peer-to-peer video sharing, and that it had 30 days to disclose its present and intended future management practices to the FCC, and submit a plan to show how it was going to end the offending practices by the end of the year.[24] In September 2009, FCC Chairman Julius Genachowski proposed two additional rules on top of its 2005 policy statement. He proposed a *non-discrimination principle* that ISPs must not discriminate against any content or applications, and a *transparency principle* that ISPs must disclose all their policies to customers. Importantly, he also argued that wireless should be subject to the same network neutrality as line providers.[25]

On June 6th, 2010, the U.S. Court of Appeal for the District of Columbia overruled the FCC.[26] The FCC has no jurisdiction over the management practices of a telecommunications corporation. After this ruling, the FCC ability to defend net neutrality was weakened. However, in December 21, 2010, the FCC announced new rules to prevent cable television and telephone service providers (such as Comcast) from blocking access to competitors (such as Netflix). But, as "a compromise" (due to pressure from Comcast, Verizon, and AT&T) the FCC changed the regulations, allowing the restriction of Internet access from mobile smartphones and tablet computers. The compromise basically bought some time for net neutrality, while ISPs gradually shift their services over to wireless. With their foot in the door of ownership over the Internet, Comcast, Verizon, and AT&T can now challenge the FCC's authority to regulate ISPs in any way. Corporations like Comcast, Verizon, and AT&T are seeking to create a tiered Internet that favors corporations and governments, and those able to pay the high fees to use it, as well as granting themselves the power to stop others from using it.[27] Under the pretexts of "copyright infringement" and "national security", Congress is about to give this power to them. Corporate media have been quite silent on this matter, yet, through the Internet, information about this has been shared, resulting in a public backlash. Despite petitions and protests, however, Congress continues to grant telecom giants more power, and the FCC has been made toothless and redundant by the Courts. In recent years, the FCC has pushed for further deregulation of all media, which, of course, does not mean that there are fewer rules, but more rules that now favor corporations. Fortunes and careers are at stake, along with an Internet that is widely and easily accessible by people, all around the world.

All of these new rules will result in increased costs to access and use the Internet—thereby reducing the democratic potential of the Internet to act as a media of the people, by the people, and for the people. The significance of this extends far beyond the use of social network and video sharing sites, like Facebook and YouTube, as well as personal sites and blogs, where people to make and share their own media. It extends to the use of the Internet as the people's media. The Internet provides the means for people to communicate, share knowledge and sources of information, educate themselves, and organize campaigns, protests, and direct action, in order to act as a democratic counter-balance to government and corporate power.

Companies already use deep packet inspection technology to identify sources and types of data, as well as reconstruct content.[28] While there may well be a technical justification for prioritizing one kind of data over another—say prioritizing video over emails, given that a few seconds delay in an email is unlikely to matter—this is a smokescreen. The aim of these new laws and treaties is to do away with net neutrality, even between the same kinds of data—treating any video data packet equally regardless of its source or destination. By effectively slowing data transmission—artificially—and charging tolls to use "the fast lane," the content of the Internet will gradually become controlled by corporations, and the fewer and fewer people who own them. The Internet will go the same way as radio and television. When using wireless devices, telecom corporations can extort higher fees from companies such as Yahoo!, Google, or Amazon, and users who did not pay these fees would either be relegated to "the slow lane" or even blocked from using the Internet. Furthermore, with the already deregulated opportunities for telecom giants such as Comcast to buy and control media corporations such as NBC, along with movie producers such as Universal, which also owns Hulu, the telecom giant can restrict or block wireless access to competitors, such as Netflix, in order to create a monopoly or to charge competitors a higher fee for video streaming. They could charge extremely high fees for downloading from any site that they do not own. Online innovations in digital media could be seriously stifled or suppressed if they competed with such corporations. Telecom corporations could block Skype or future innovations in Internet based communications that compete with their phone services. By controlling the data pipeline, telecom giants would be not only be in a position to impose a tiered structure on data transmission speed and also prioritize types of data, allowing them to create artificial scarcity and justify charging even higher fees for their services, but the opportunities for political abuse are rife if powerful moneyed interests are able to act as gatekeepers and shut down websites or networks they do not like or which compete with their subsidiaries or journalists who report on events involving their corporate interests.

Corporations such as Qwest, Comcast, AT&T, Time Warner, and Verizon spend millions of dollars lobbying Congress to further weaken the FCC and to do away with net neutrality and any restrictions on their control over the Internet. They also spend millions of dollars on Astroturf groups to misinform people and convince politicians that there is public opposition to net neutrality and the FCC. This kind of influence is particularly troubling when those corporations can come to agreements to divide up broadcasting and mobile coverage, thereby forming a trust and avoiding any competition, leading to higher prices, poorer service, and higher profits. This kind of agreement is the reason why anti-trust legislation is necessary and it is the job of Congress and the FCC to enforce it. While competition could be ensured without needed further regulation, if Congress allowed the Internet to be classified as a utility, it is in the interests of citizens that their government prevents monopolistic practices by telecoms corporations.

If we hope for any possibility of democracy, we need to raise our voices and organize to defend the principle of net neutrality. Supporters of net neutrality include Vinton Cerf (co-inventor of the Internet at the Defense Advanced Research Projects Agency (DARPA) along with Bob Kahn) and Tim Berners-Lee (inventor of the World Wide Web at CERN). Supporters of net neutrality also range from corporations like Yahoo!, Google, Microsoft, and other high-tech Silicon Valley companies to disparate groups such as Free Press, savetheinternet.com, MoveOn.org, the Service Employees Union, the National Religious Broadcasters, the American Library Association, the Community Legal Defense Fund. Even Glenn Beck, now that he has left the bosom of corporate media—CNN and Fox News—to restart his own career as an online televangelist on the Internet-based GBTV, has changed his tune from opposing and misrepresenting net neutrality, to defending it and denouncing proposed laws, such as SOPA and PIPA.[29] Yet corporate media, including Fox News, MSNBC, and CNN have remained conspicuously silent about proposed Senate and House bills, and the proposed rule changes by the new FCC chair Ajit Pai, leaving reporting and protest to the Internet. Similarly, corporate media has been conspicuously silent about ACTA, its significance, and the mass protests against it throughout Europe, especially in Germany, the Netherlands, and the United Kingdom. It has also remain silent about the proposed mergers of giant media conglomerates and the effect this will have on Internet ownership and access.

The Internet itself provides the means by which many grassroots organizations and public groups comprised of ordinary Internet users come together and defend net neutrality. People are concerned about how the loss of net neutrality would restrict their access to the Internet and stifle freedom of speech, democracy, knowledge, innovation, and also free-market competition. Net neutrality has protected free-market competition on the Internet and brought many undeniable benefits as a result of allowing people to start up their own Internet businesses with a computer and access to the Internet. It also brings with it the real possibility that any Internet site could have the reach of a TV or radio station, which allows public media to counterbalance corporate media, hence counter the problems caused by the Citizens United ruling and the corporate domination of corporate media coverage of the political process and elections. The loss of net neutrality would end this unparalleled opportunity for freedom of expression, especially political speech.[30] It would also end the opportunity for people to peacefully petition their government through the Internet, without that petition being filtered or blocked in accordance with corporate interests. This is particularly important when people are trying to share knowledge and organize to protest corporate dominance over government policy, especially when it involves government policy about how to respond to the right of the people to assemble and petition their government. It is for this reason that net neutrality has been eroded by politicians and their corporate sponsors. Although to be fair, some politicians have also recognized the importance of net neutrality and have tried to pass laws to protect it. Senator Byron Dorgan introduced a bill S215 in 2007, now called the Internet Freedom Act, which would amend the 1934 Communications Act to compel ISPs to guarantee net neutrality.[31] This bill has been read twice and has been referred to the Committee on Science, Commerce, and Transportation, where it has remained until 2015, when Senator Mike Lee (R-Utah) introduced the Restoring Internet Freedom Act that would greatly restrict the regulatory powers of the FCC, and a new version of the Internet Freedom Act was introduced by Senator Ted Cruz (R-Texas), which would effectively end net neutrality and prevent the FCC from passing rules, such as treating the Internet as a utility or classifying ISPs as "common carrier" under the Communications Act.

Corporate media have not just rested at remaining silent about the imminent threat to net neutrality, but the propaganda machine has been turned aggressively against net neutrality. With the propaganda machine in full force, lobbyists fully mobilized, and the Super PACs fully funded, only a well informed and organized public will be able to resist the treat to net neutrality by using the Internet to defend itself. The struggle for the future of the Internet is upon us. Defenders of these telecom giants, argue that this is simply a property rights issue. If ISPs own access to the Internet, and these ISPs are investing in new technologies such as fiber optic infrastructure, isn't net neutrality a violation of property rights? This question does raise a very important point. People may petition and protest the erosion of net neutrality, but unless the FCC can enforce its rule and defend this principle, or Congress is willing to pass legislation to do so, neither of which seem likely, telecom giants will get their way because they own the access to the Internet.

It is for this reason that we need a public ISP, so that the public can own the infrastructure to access the Internet, thereby providing competition to the telecom giants and allowing net neutrality to be preserved, and even providing low cost or free access to public schools and libraries. Under Article I, Congress has the constitutional authority and obligation to "establish post offices and post roads" and to "promote the progress of science and the useful arts." Arguably, both of these powers could be extended to the Internet and provide the legal basis for the creation of a public ISP run by the US Postal Service. This would also allow the services offered by the USPS to incorporate new technologies, facilitate communication, and satisfy public needs, and allow the USPS to adapt to a changing world. This would fulfill Congress's constitutional obligation to establish post offices and post roads, and allow for the nation to develop its communication technologies through both its public and private sectors. Just as defenders of the Second Amendment would scoff at claims that their right to bear arms was limited to muskets, canons, and swords, it would be equally ridiculous to claim that Congress's Article I obligation was limited to the communication technology of the eighteenth century and the delivery of letters and parcels. Publicly owned Internet access also allows Congress to fulfill its obligation to protect intellectual

30

property rights, promote science and the useful arts, and provide for the common defense and general welfare. As well as benefiting Americans by keepings costs down and providing a high level of customer service, it would also mean that the public would have its own national communications network, available for emergencies, which would provide additional national security. An advanced public telecommunications sector would provide training and employment as well.

In this way, not only could Congress and the FCC avoid many of the problems caused by regulation and its enforcement, but a public ISP operated by the USPS would give the public an alternative means of accessing the Internet, increasing market competition, and imposing market discipline on the management practices of telecom giants. It would also provide a route by which the FCC could apply eminent domain should privately owned ISPs fail to provide the public affordable means to access the Internet. But, in most part, people would simply be able to switch to the public ISP should they become dissatisfied with their current ISP. By offering a genuine public sector solution, market competition could act as a counterbalance to the monopolistic practices of telecom giants, without requiring excessive regulation or government oversight over private management practices, and people would be able to choose between public access to the Internet based on net neutrality or a tiered Internet service provided by telecom giants. This would mean that the FCC would have a means of defending net neutrality and allow for the further deregulation of the private sector, thereby satisfying the public need for the means to communicate, without stifling innovation or interfering with business management practices. Such a public ISP would also be able to pay for itself and offer low cost access to the public. The telecom giants could not reasonably object to this, if we are to take seriously their claim that a tiered Internet is necessary for the improvement of quality of service, because it would be left to the public to decide for themselves whether they preferred private or public Internet access. If the spokespeople for the telecom giants are correct, the public will continue to use their ISPs and not switch to a public ISP.

The USPS is an independent government agency that has a long history dating back to the beginning of the United States of America.

The USPS was founded in 1775 by the Second Continental Congress, and in 1792 the Post Office Department was established by the first U.S. Congress, with Benjamin Franklin as the first Postmaster General.[32] Until telegraph lines were privatized in 1847, they had been owned by the public and the Post Office Department operated them. The USPS was modernized by the 1971 Postal Reorganization Act. Despite being self-funding since the 1980s, in recent years the USPS has lost revenue due to a decline in mail volume, as people are increasingly using the Internet. It is also the case that the 2006 Postal Accountability and Enhancement Act, which obligated the USPS to pre-fund 75 years of health care coverage for each retired postal worker (a requirement that is not imposed on any other government agency), has caused budgetary problems for the USPS. In November 2011, it was announced that in May 2012 almost 30,000 jobs will be lost and over 250 post offices will be closed. If the USPS were able to operate as a public ISP, this would provide much needed revenue, as well as offer new jobs, training, and low-cost Internet access to the public, as well as continue its current postal services. As the telecom giants move more of their business into wireless connections and creating a tiered Internet, the USPS could take over the land lines and provide ISP services to public schools and libraries free of charge, allow for low cost extension of NPR and PBS, and public access stations, and be regulated by Congress and the FCC to preserve net neutrality. A USPS-run and publicly owned national ISP could complement the services of municipal and state owned networks to provide national coverage in competition with the telecom giants.

Acting as an alternative to corporate media, cooperation between the USPS, PBS, and NPR, offering a national network of national, state, and local community stations and ISP, would balance corporate media and correct the Citizens United v FEC ruling, without requiring any new regulations over corporate media or overturning Citizens United. Run according to the principle of net neutrality, under the scrutiny and regulatory jurisdiction of both the FCC and FEC during primaries and elections, public media could offer the people high quality coverage of elections—across the nation. This coverage would be consistent with BCRA in that all political candidates would get equal time and the right to respond to any comment made about them by any other candidate. Coverage of elections and the political process would be conducted without editorializing or commentary—restricted to the reporting of events and facts. Fair and open coverage of political candidates being interviewed and questioned is very healthy for a democracy.

However, it seems almost a flight of fantasy to consider any such possibility of a public ISP under a Republican controlled Congress, as we see its willingness to end net neutrality and turn the Internet over to the telecom giants. Furthermore, with cuts to NPR and PBS underway, the future of public media in general looks bleak.

Could something resembling net neutrality be defended using 'soft' regulation such as the Fairness Doctrine? This legal principle means that balance should be respected by media, at least during election campaigns, by giving all candidates equal time and their right to reply, fully, without editing, commentary, or censorship. If candidates wish to spend their available time running campaign ads or issue advocacy ads, they should be free to do so, providing that they clearly state their endorsement of those ads and credit their sources of funding for any ads they endorse. Any other candidate mentioned by name should have equal time available for a reply. Surely candidates would demonstrate their powers of brevity and succinctness, and if a candidate is not available to reply, their time should remain available to them right up to the election, and should they refuse to reply then that could be reported as a matter of fact. The FCC and FEC would have no jurisdiction over the content of political speech, simply over media access and time. The FCC would simply make sure that equal treatment of data transmission and user-impartial telecommunication took place; the FEC would make sure that every registered political candidate had equal treatment. The First Amendment right to free speech would be respected and so the Supreme Court need not be involved; it would provide a needed public service without costing the taxpayer a dime, and so Congress should be content with it. FEC jurisdiction would ensure that public standards of broadcasting were upheld. These standards should be those of equality and fairness, impartiality and decency. However, whatever content users uploaded onto this publicly owned Internet would be unrestricted in its content (with obvious exceptions, such as child pornography, terrorist communications, or any other federally illegal material) and free speech would be respected. The only constraints would be those imposed by the limits of the available technology for speed and quantity of data transmission. All of it could all be paid for by public donations, USPS charges, and revenues from commercial advertising. It could also provide a medium for the federal or state governments to provide information about public services and emergencies. Yet, again, it doesn't seem likely that Congress would do any of this.

There clearly are public benefits to be had from owning public media that provides affordable and accessible high quality multi-media services and opportunities to participate in their further development. Through the USPS, PBS, and NPR, the public could maintain and develop a nationwide communications network, a strong public sector of technically skilled and unionized workers, and opportunities for participation in the political process. With the ability to cooperate with other networks, global connection with the Internet would be available to anyone, allowing people to communicate, learn, share experiences and ideas, as well as news and information, and own and develop their own media, all of which are vital for the future of democracy worldwide. In the age of electronic data transmission and multimedia politics, net neutrality safeguards the infrastructure of the democratic process.

Otherwise, how can there be any legitimate basis for any international criticism of governments that control and censor Internet use? These governments can claim that they are only censoring illegal data too. How can anyone criticize the government of the People's Republic of China for restricting the dissemination of information and shutting down websites if the Western governments and corporations do it as well? Imposing excessive restrictions in the name of "copyright infringement" will also legitimate the methods by which totalitarian and oppressive regimes control information and dissent. Yet if we look at the Internet in countries such as China and Egypt, or Turkey, we can see how it has in fact empowered political dissent and helped people to organize democratic protests against government tyranny and oppression, as well as provide an alternative to ideological or religious fundamentalism. It has also allowed the rest of the world to learn about the conditions of people under these tyrannical governments. Western media corporations avoid covering acts of ethnic cleansing and political and religious oppression in China and Tibet so as to avoid the risk of offending the government of China, and risk losing favor in their access to the growing media market of China. Yet, via the Internet, Chinese people are able to communicate with the people around the world and tell them what is happening in China. If media and telecom conglomerates have monopolistic control over access to the Internet, what would stop them from preventing Chinese dissidents from communicating with the outside world, if compliance with the demands of the Chinese government was a condition for making commercial arrangements and gaining access to a massive market? Nothing. They could also suppress all coverage throughout corporate media about having done so as well. It would be as if those dissenters never existed, while corporate media pundits inform us that the Chinese government is undertaking vital free-market reforms.

What can people do? People can use the Internet to better inform themselves and connect with like-minded others to petition their government. Even though the FCC no longer enforces an Open Internet Policy, people can file a complaint with the FCC if their ISP has unfairly prevented access to the Internet or charges tolls to access specific websites. People can also write to the FCC to express their support for this policy and net neutrality, as well as write to their members of Congress and the state legislature, and also the President about the need for public media to cover elections and the political process. These is only a very narrow window of time for people to do this, as both Congress and the FCC are advancing their agenda of eroding and ending both open access and net neutrality. People can also point out that public media is important for national security and for the federal and state governments to provide information during an emergency. People can write to newspapers, share information through social networks, and join Internet-based campaigns in defense of net neutrality, as well as calling for a public ISP. People could also write the postal workers unions—the National Association of Letter Carriers (NALC), the National Rural Letter Carriers' Association (NRLCA), and the National Postal Mail Handlers Union (NPMHU)—to give their support for the USPS and for a USPS-run ISP.

If we agree that the Internet and net neutrality are essential for "the public interest, convenience, and necessity" it is vital for the public to resist and counterbalance the domination of mass media by media corporations. Public participation in mass media does not just require net neutrality. It requires affordable public access to media, including PBS and NPR and a public ISP. The public needs to participate in the generation and transmission of public debate and education—the dissemination of knowledge, ideas, skills, inspiration, and intelligence—and also engage in the political process. The recent FCC decision to scrap the applications for corporate media repeater stations (which repeat nationally syndicated radio shows) and allow local community radio stations to apply for these licenses instead is a very positive step in the right direction.[33] What is now needed is a combination of tighter protections of net neutrality from Congress and the FCC, along with better funding of an independent public media.

Independent public media is necessary for the public to oversee and question the activities of government agencies, effectively petition government, and elect people who represent them. It is for this reason that both net neutrality and public media are necessary for the future of democracy. However, people do not have to wait for the government to fulfill its obligation to protect net neutrality and the public interest. We can build and use our own Internet. One such project to do this is the Free Network Foundation started by Isaac Wilder using a wireless network of radio towers.[34] This is akin to using pirate radio to create a mobile and impromptu decentralized network—called a mesh network—which can not only provide people with their own ISP, but do so in a way that it is impossible for any government or corporation to control, switch off, or spy upon. It is one of the many examples of how available technologies can be appropriated for democratic purposes to provide the physical infrastructure for democratic media. This may well be vital for the future of a democratic Internet, the preservation of public access media, and the real potential for the dissemination and development of genuinely alternative media. This kind of mobile technology and impromptu network may well be vital for the future of democracy in America and the rest of the world. Any successful campaign against corporate and government control over the media must have its own alternative media to disseminate information and coordinate activities. And that alternative media is the free press. However, it is likely that Congress will pass laws to criminalize such networks and technologies.

People need to stop trusting the images, spin, and sound bites fed to them by corporate media. We should switch off the media pundits and propagandists! As customers, as workers, and as investors people do retain a great deal of power in the marketplace *if we organize* to shape corporate policy through boycotts, unionization, strikes, conscientious investment, and changing our patterns of consumption—including changing channels or switching off the TV or radio. But this kind of activity can only be effective as part of larger citizens' mass movements and campaigns to democratize America through grassroots organization and political action; using the Internet to inform and enroll others, as well as being informed and enrolled by others, as a popular mass movement to create democratic mass media.

This is democracy in action, which is only possible only if the people stand up and assert the right to self-governance through democratic political institutions and organizations to participate in making decisions about in how their country is governed and for whom. Democracy is at stake. A democracy is won or lost by the people. It is never given to the people, as a coming-of-age present. Democracy happens when people wake up, organize, and become a democracy, from the people, by the people, and for the people. Only the people can do this.

The situation is stark, but far from hopeless. In many respects, we are witnessing a repeat of the 1870s Gilded Age when the wealthy elite owned newspapers and rode roughshod over the political institutions of that time and used them to get richer and defend their own interests at the expense of everyone else. Grassroots movements of farmers, workers, and reformers rose up and heralded what became known as the Progressive Era. It was joined by unions, along with churches, charities, and a few politicians. This progressive movement was either ignored or vilified by the press of their day (just as the progressive movement has been mistreated by corporate media today). Progressive Era campaigners had to create their own newspapers (what became the Reform Press Association) and set up a network of thousands of public speakers who traveled across America, spreading ideas and bringing news, and expanding their movement and networks across America from town to town, city to city, state to state. Today, the Internet provides the possibility of grassroots political campaigns being organized by any group of citizens with access to computers and a server. Today, through the Internet, we are almost seeing history repeat itself, except on a much larger scale across America and throughout the world. These online activities are combined with protests, petitions, cooperatives, meetings, movies, books, art, music, and theatre to create a powerful alternative to corporate media. This alternative media reaches, inspires, and enrolls millions of people daily.

We are witnessing the rebirth and growth of a powerful, progressive, and critical alternative media, perhaps possessed of the spirit that the delegates at the Philadelphia Convention in 1787 had in mind when they considered the First Amendment and the press. Media reform is necessary for realizing and continuing the American Revolution—the ongoing experiment in self-governance. By being vigilant against and critical towards abuses of governmental and corporate power, with the ability to organize campaigns and movements against those abuses, and to keep the representatives of the people honest and accountable to the people, the citizenry can use the Internet to democratize the media, by becoming the media. The First Amendment favors political speech. Vigilant, critical, passionate, and democratic participation by citizens in the institutions of government is necessary for democracy, and it is the way that the American people can finally achieve a government by themselves, of themselves, and for themselves.

This is why the Internet is a valuable resource and net neutrality is essential. Today, anyone with a computer, a modem, and an ISP can connect to the Internet and become part of "the free press." The Internet is a participatory and interactive medium. Add decentralized, grassroots communication and organization of millions of people into the fray and we have the real possibility of democracy ahead of us.

[1] Brian Stelter, "Netflix Partner Says Comcast 'Toll' Threatens Online Video Delivery", *The New York Times*, Nov, 29, 2010 http://mediadecoder.blogs.nytimes.com/2010/11/29/netflix-partner-says-comcast-toll-threatens-online-video-delivery/?ref=technology and Marguerite Reardon, "Level 3 Takes Spat with Comcast Public", *CNET News*, Nov, 29, 2011 http://news.cnet.com/8301-1023_3-20024070-93.html. See also Seth Weintraub, "With Demands on Level 3, Comcast Ups Its Flight With Netflix", *CNN*, Nov, 30, 2010 http://tech.fortune.cnn.com/2010/11/30/now-showing-comcast-previews-a-world-without-net-neutrality/ .

[2] Robert W. McChesney, *Corporate Media and the Threat to Democracy*. (Seven Stories Press, 1997); Joe Harper & Thom Yantek, ed., *Media, Profit, and Politics: Competing Priorities in an Open Society*. (Kent State University Press, 2003); Benjamin H. Bagdikian, *The New Media Monopoly*. (Beacon Press, 2004) ; David Skinner, ed., *Converging Media, Diverging Politics: A Political Economy of News Media in the United States and Canada*. (Lexington Books, 2005); David Croteau and William Hoynes, *The Business of Media: Corporate Media and the Public Interest*. (Pine Forge Press, 2006); Edwin C. Baker, *Media Concentration and Democracy: Why Ownership Matters*. (Cambridge University Press, 2007); Amelia H. Arsenault and Manuel Castells, "The Structure and Dynamics of Global Multi-Media Business Networks" *International Journal of Communication, Vol 2* (2008); Eli M. Noam, *Media Ownership and Concentration in America*, (Oxford University Press, 2009); Anup Shah, "Media Conglomerates, Mergers, Concentration of Ownership", *Global Issues*, (Jan, 2, 2009) http://www.globalissues.org/article/159/media-conglomerates-mergers-concentration-of-ownership; For a chart showing the history of media ownership published by *Mother Jones* see http://motherjones.com/files/legacy/news/feature/2007/03/and_then_the re_were_eight.pdf See also the 2004 documentary *Orwell Rolls In His Grave* http://orwellrollsinhisgrave.com/

[3] For their website go to: http://www.opensecrets.org/

[4] For the original story see http://www.nytimes.com/1983/01/21/nyregion/the-region-ge-plant-accused-of-water-pollution.html?n=Top%2fReference%2fTimes%2fSubjects %2fW%2fWater%20Pollution;

See also Thomas F. O'Boyle, *At Any Cost: Jack Welch, General Electric, and the Pursuit of Profit* (Vintage Press, 1999). This was confirmed by the Justice Department (Oct, 7, 1999).
http://www.justice.gov/opa/pr/1999/October/471enr.htm.
Environmental Protection Agency report and updates http://www.epa.gov/hudson/; and the Natural Resources Defense Council report and updates http://www.nrdc.org/water/pollution/hhudson.asp.

[5] Bain Capital owns Clear Channel Communications—Bain Capital is the company formerly run by the former GOP presidential candidate Mitt Romney. It seems reasonable to ask whether the on air tirades by conservative radio talk show hosts have been orchestrated against Romney's opponents and any criticisms of Bain Capital. See John Kiesewetter, "Mitt Romney, Bain Capital, and Clear Channel Communications" *Cincinnati.com*, Jan, 12, 2012
http://cincinnati.com/blogs/tv/2012/01/12/mitt-romey-bain-capital-and-clear-channel/

[6] Kelo v. City of New London, 545 US 469 (2005)

[7] Diane Renzuli and the Center for Public Integrity, *Capital Offenders: How Private Interests Govern Our States* (Washington, DC: Public Integrity Books, 2002); Lee Drutman and Charlie Cray, *The People's Business: Controlling Corporations and Restoring Democracy* (Berrett-Koehler, 2004)

[8] For numerous examples see media watchdogs Media Matters for America http://mediamatters.org/ and Fox News Lies
http://foxnewslies.net/

[9] Buckley v Valeo, 424 U.S. 1 (1976)

[10] Citizens United v FEC 130 US 876 (2010)

[11] Ownership of media in a given market is now permitted up to 45% of that market; there are no restrictions on newspaper and TV station ownership in the same market; all radio and TV channels, magazines, newspapers, cable, and Internet services are included in the FCC "diversity index", regardless of whether they offer news or not; and licenses are no longer reviewed for "public-interest" considerations.

[12] Free Press website: http://www.freepress.net/

[13] Robert McChesney, "Understanding the Media Reform Movement", *International Journal of Communication* **3**: 51., 2009; An interview with Robert McChesney, "Media Capitalism, the State and 21st Century Media Democracy Struggles" *The Bullet*, E-bulletin No. 246, Aug, 9, 2009
http://www.socialistproject.ca/bullet/246.php

[14] The Prometheus Radio Project website:
http://www.prometheusradio.org/

40

[15] Fairness & Accuracy In Reporting, March, 1, 2002, "Media Giants Cast Aside Regulatory Chains: FCC should resist attempt to gut ownership restrictions" http://www.fair.org/activism/fcc-giants.html]

[16] S. 968: Preventing Real Online Threats to Economic Creativity and Theft of Intellectual Property Act http://www.govtrack.us/congress/bills/112/s968
H.R. 3261: Stop Online Piracy Act http://www.govtrack.us/congress/bills/112/hr3261;
S. 2105: Cybersecurity Act of 2012 http://www.govtrack.us/congress/bills/112/s2105 See also Gerry Smith, "Cybersecurity Bill Faces Uncertain Future In Fight Over Regulation," *Huffington Post*, Mar, 19, 2012 http://www.huffingtonpost.com/2012/03/19/cybersecurity-bill-regulation_n_1362529.html

[17] Anti-Counterfeiting Trade Agreement http://www.ustr.gov/acta ; Emily Glen, "ACTA: A SOPA By Any Other Name," *Urban Times*, Feb, 3, 2012
 http://www.theurbn.com/2012/02/acta-sopa-pipa/

[18] See Rogers, K., *Debunking Glenn Beck: How to Save America from Media Pundits and Propagandists* (Santa Barbara, CA: Praeger, 2011), Chapter 12

[19] Robert Kahn and Ed Feigenbaum, "An Evening with Robert Kahn" at the Computer History Museum, California, January 9th, 2007. A partial transcript of this discussion can be found at http://vasarely.wiwi.hu-berlin.de/kahn_net_neutrality_transcript.html The first network utilizing the basic protocols of the Internet was launched January 1, 1983 on ARPANET—a government run and public funded network. Since the beginning of its commercial use in the 1990s, the Internet has become complex and vast in scale. The Internet today is defined heavily by its interconnections and routing policies, to which the principle of net neutrality applies.

[20] See *Debunking Glenn Beck*, Chap. 12

[21] Tim Wu, *Network Neutrality FAQ*:
http://timwu.org/network_neutrality.html

[22] FCC Policy Statement (FCC 05-151)
http://fjallfoss.fcc.gov/edocs_public/attachmatch/FCC-05-151A1.pdf

[23] Peter Svensson, "Comcast Blocks Some Internet Traffic," *Associated Press*, Sep, 19, 2007
http://www.msnbc.msn.com/id/21376597/#.TzTmpsXlNMU; *Reuters* Feb, 25, 2008 http://www.reuters.com/article/2008/02/25/us-internet-fcc-idUSN2525077120080225

[24] Aaron K. Brauer-Riek, "The FCC Tackles Net Neutrality: Agency Jurisdiction and the Comcast Order," *Berkeley Technology Law Journal* 24:1, 2009

[25] Tim Greene, "What's the FCC ruling all about?" *Network World*, Oct, 22, 2009 http://www.networkworld.com/news/2009/102209-fcc-net-neutrality.html

[26] Comcast Corp. v FCC, 600 F.3d 642, 2010

[27] Jesse Hamilton, "AT&T Must Let Beastie Boy Vote on Net Neutrality, SEC Says," *Bloomberg Businessweek*, Feb, 16, 2012 http://www.businessweek.com/news/2012-02-16/at-t-must-let-beastie-boy-vote-on-net-neutrality-sec-says.html

[28] Nate Anderson, "Deep Packet Inspection Meets Net Neutrality," Ars Technica, 25th July, 2007, http://arstechnica.com/hardware/news/2007/07/Deep-packet-inspection-meets-net-neutrality.ars/2

[29] GBTV, Jan, 18, 2012: http://www.glennbeck.com/2012/01/18/glenn-wait-pipa-isnt-kate-middletons-sister/

[30] Lawrence Lessig and Robert McChesney, "No Tolls on The Internet," *Washington Post*, June, 8, 2006 http://www.washingtonpost.com/wp-dyn/content/article/2006/06/07/AR2006060702108.html

[31] See Library of Congress Bill Summary & Status webpage: http://thomas.loc.gov/cgi-bin/bdquery/z?d110:S.215:

[32] Lindsay Rogers, *The Postal Power of Congress* (BiblioLife, 2009), first published 1923

[33] Stephen C. Webster, "FCC Decision Strikes Critical Blow to Right-Wing Radio Dominance," *The Raw Story*, Mar, 20, 2012 http://www.rawstory.com/rs/2012/03/20/fcc-decision-strikes-critical-blow-to-right-wing-radio-dominance/ See the FCC website: http://transition.fcc.gov/Daily_Releases/Daily_Business/2012/db0319/DOC-313080A1.pdf and for help in setting up a local community radio station and applying for a license see the Prometheus Radio Project website: http://www.prometheusradio.org/

[34] The Free Network Foundation website: http://freenetworkfoundation.org/ See also the 2012 documentary *Free the Network* directed by Brian Anderson http://motherboard.vice.com/2012/3/28/motherboard-tv-free-the-network; Keith Wagstaff "Occupy the Internet: Protests Give Rise to DIY Networks," *Time*, Mar, 28, 2012

www.ingramcontent.com/pod-product-compliance
Lightning Source LLC
Chambersburg PA
CBHW062026280526
45787CB00005B/2231